Light
and
Shadows

CONTENTS

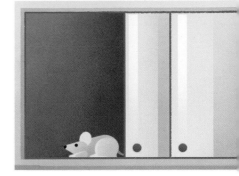
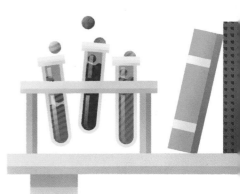

THE SCIENTIFIC METHOD

The **SCIENTIFIC METHOD** is the way in which **SCIENCE** investigates the **REALITY** around us. It is the most reliable method we know to progress in the **KNOWLEDGE** of things and of the world.

Scientific does not mean "accurate"; instead, it means something is **reproducible**, that is, that it can be repeated. With the same initial conditions, we expect the experiment to always have the same result. The scientific method is **EXPERIMENTAL**, that is, based on experiments, tests, and observations, and this is the fun part in which the scientist becomes creative!

THE MAIN STAGES OF EXPERIMENTAL SCIENTIFIC METHOD ARE:

1. Observing a phenomenon and asking yourself questions.
2. Formulating a hypothesis, that is, a possible explanation of the phenomenon.
3. Carrying out an experiment to check if the hypothesis is correct.
4. Analyzing the results.
5. Repeating the experiment in different ways.
6. Coming to a conclusion and establishing a rule.

"What we know is a drop; what we don't know is an ocean!"

TRAVELING WITH YOU!

You can call me **PROF. ALBERT**.
I'm a renowned scientist and a lover
of outdoor trips and cycling.
I'm passionate about life,
the universe, and...everything!

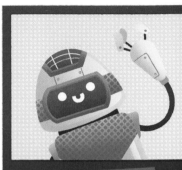

I'm **GREG** the **ROBOT**,
an advanced form
of artificial intelligence.
I have a positronic
brain with too many
mistakes in it.

My name is **MONICA**.
I love traveling
and reading books.
I am really passionate
about cooking.

TWO WORDS: SAFETY FIRST!

1. Before doing any experiment, always read all the instructions carefully and make sure you have all the materials you need to do it.

2. It is forbidden to eat or drink during the experiments and, above all, to eat or drink your experiment! It's a bad idea! Don't do it.

3. Use old clothes because you will get dirty!

4. Wash your hands after every experiment. Some substances you use may be harmful to your health.

5. For some of the experiments it is important to try them several times in order to master them. Supervising adults should allow kids to experiment, make mistakes, and try again.

6. Always clean your utensils after you've finished an experiment or project, and make sure you put them away tidily.

7. Throw away any garbage or substances in the correct trash can.

Some of the scientific activities in the book require adult supervision.

All the words in CAPITAL LETTERS are in the Glossary on pages 46–47, where the terms are explained in more detail.

LIGHT IS LIFE!

Light is life, heat, energy.
Thanks to light, for example, plants perform photosynthesis
to live, and solar panels transform
light energy into electricity.

AS FAST AS LIGHT

In a vacuum, light travels in a straight line at a speed of approximately 186,000 miles/second (300,000 km/s)!

Light takes about 8 minutes to travel from the sun to Earth, covering about 93 million miles (150 million km).

LIGHT AND SHADOWS

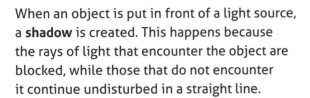

When an object is put in front of a light source, a **shadow** is created. This happens because the rays of light that encounter the object are blocked, while those that do not encounter it continue undisturbed in a straight line.

An object illuminated by a **point** light **source** produces a **clear shadow**.

An object illuminated by a **wider** light **source** produces a **blurrier shadow**.

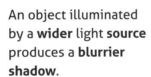

7

SHADOWS ON THE WALL

HOW TO DO IT

1 Cut out any shape you like from the cardboard, using scissors. It can be abstract or realistic.

YOU WILL NEED

- a flashlight
- a table lamp
- cardboard
- a dark room
- scissors
- a wooden skewer
- Scotch tape

2 Attach the skewer to the cardboard shape with Scotch tape.

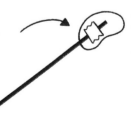

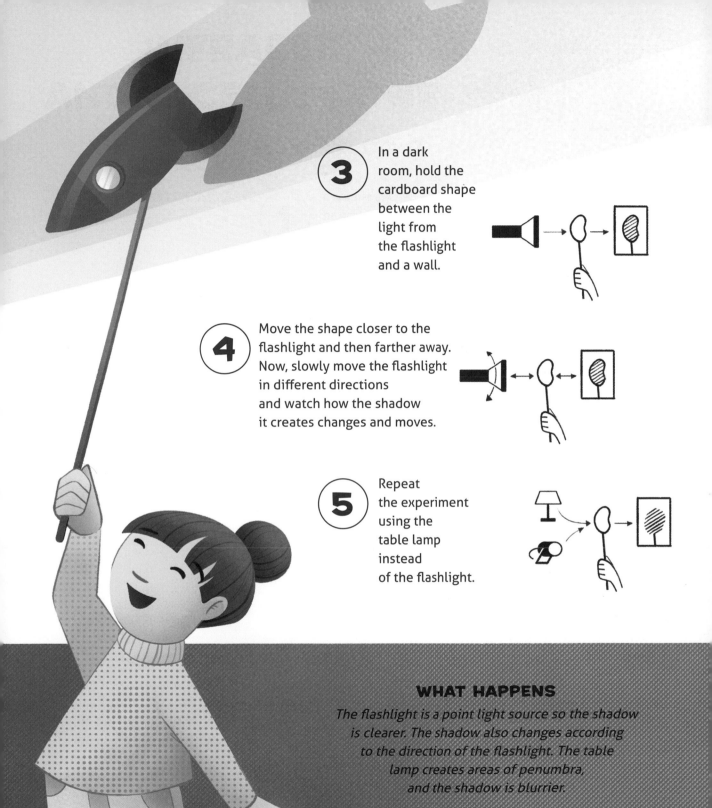

3 In a dark room, hold the cardboard shape between the light from the flashlight and a wall.

4 Move the shape closer to the flashlight and then farther away. Now, slowly move the flashlight in different directions and watch how the shadow it creates changes and moves.

5 Repeat the experiment using the table lamp instead of the flashlight.

WHAT HAPPENS

The flashlight is a point light source so the shadow is clearer. The shadow also changes according to the direction of the flashlight. The table lamp creates areas of penumbra, and the shadow is blurrier.

SHADOW PUPPETS

Now that you know how a shadow is made, as well as the best conditions to create a clear and well-defined one, try to create fantastic animals by using just your hands.

DIFFICULTY:

DIRTINESS:

TIME: *20 minutes*

DO IT WITH:

YOU WILL NEED
- *a flashlight*
- *a dark room*

HOW TO DO IT

DOG

ELEPHANT

1 Choose one of the animals suggested on this or the next page. Now, put your hands in the same position as those in the illustration.

ROOSTER

2 Find the best distance between the flashlight and the wall to create the best possible shadow.

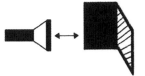

3 Try moving the animal's "mouth" and "ears" to bring it to life. You can also try making the corresponding animal noise to make it even more realistic!

BIRD

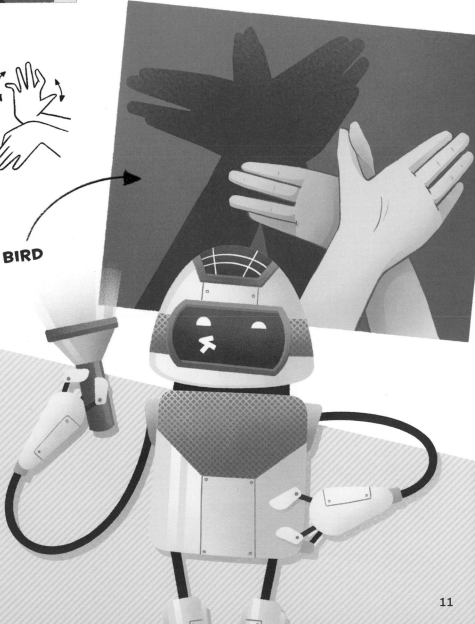

WHAT HAPPENS

By knowing the correct angle at which to hold your hands and the correct distance to keep between the flashlight and the wall, you can create the shapes of lots of different animals. Keep practicing and have fun with your friends!

11

LUMOS!

In the **HARRY POTTER** books, "Lumos" is a **spell** to create **light** when it's dark. **Lumos Solem** produces light similar to sunlight, whereas **Lumos Maxima** creates a stronger light than that of the basic spell.

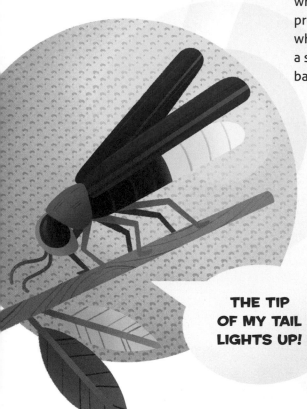

THE TIP
OF MY TAIL
LIGHTS UP!

LUMOS!

In real life, the **sun** is our main **source** of **light**, but there are also other things that emit light, for example candles, light bulbs, or the fireflies we can see on warm summer nights.

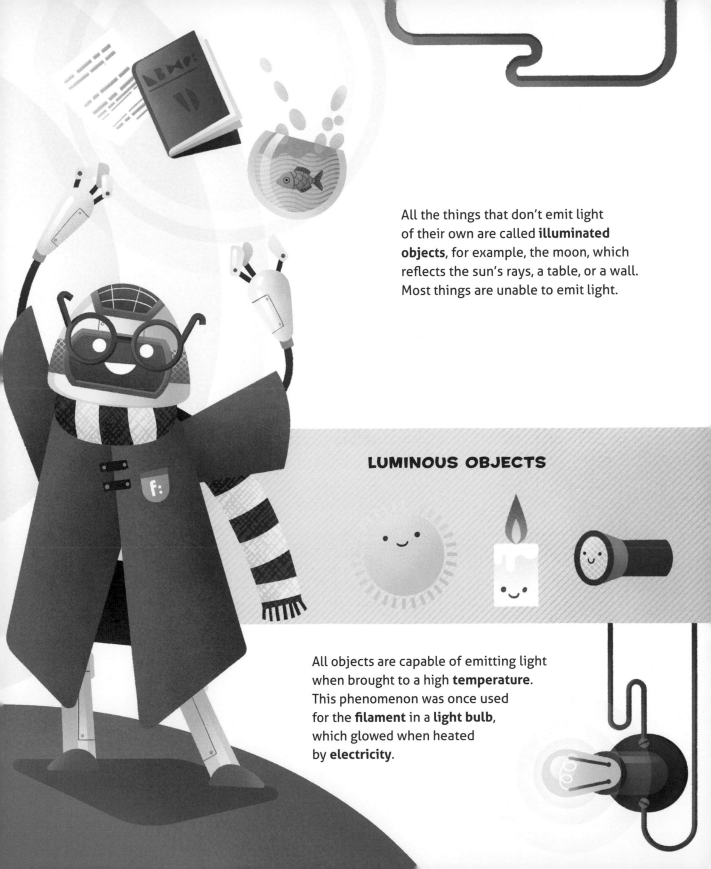

All the things that don't emit light of their own are called **illuminated objects**, for example, the moon, which reflects the sun's rays, a table, or a wall. Most things are unable to emit light.

LUMINOUS OBJECTS

All objects are capable of emitting light when brought to a high **temperature**. This phenomenon was once used for the **filament** in a **light bulb**, which glowed when heated by **electricity**.

LIGHT IN MATERIALS

When light encounters an obstacle, it changes its path. It can be deflected, slowed down, and even blocked.

OPAQUE materials block light; that is, they do not allow light to pass through them. Wood, metal, rock, and cardboard are some examples of this kind of material.

TRANSPARENT materials allow light to pass through them, making it possible to see objects clearly behind them; some examples are air, water, and glass.

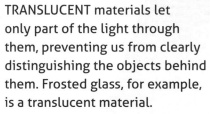

TRANSLUCENT materials let only part of the light through them, preventing us from clearly distinguishing the objects behind them. Frosted glass, for example, is a translucent material.

TESTING MATERIALS

DIRTINESS:

TIME: *5–10 minutes*

DO IT WITH:

+

HOW TO DO IT

YOU WILL NEED

- *a plastic bottle*
- *a glass*
- *a cushion*
- *a book*
- *parchment paper*
- *a portable mirror*
- *paper*
- *a pencil*

1 Put your hand inside or behind each object.

2 Using the paper and pencil, make a note about whether or not you can see your hand.

3 Classify the objects as opaque, transparent, or translucent.

Try with other materials you find around the house, then make notes of your findings.

WHAT HAPPENS

If you can see your hand clearly, the material is TRANSPARENT. If your hand is blurred and not very clear, the material is TRANSLUCENT. If you can't see your hand at all, the material is OPAQUE.

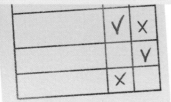

REFLECTIONS OF LIGHT

When a ray of light encounters an obstacle, two things can happen:

1. If the surface is extremely smooth, like the surface of a lake or a mirror, the rays of light are reflected in an orderly manner and the image is clear. This phenomenon is called REFLECTION.

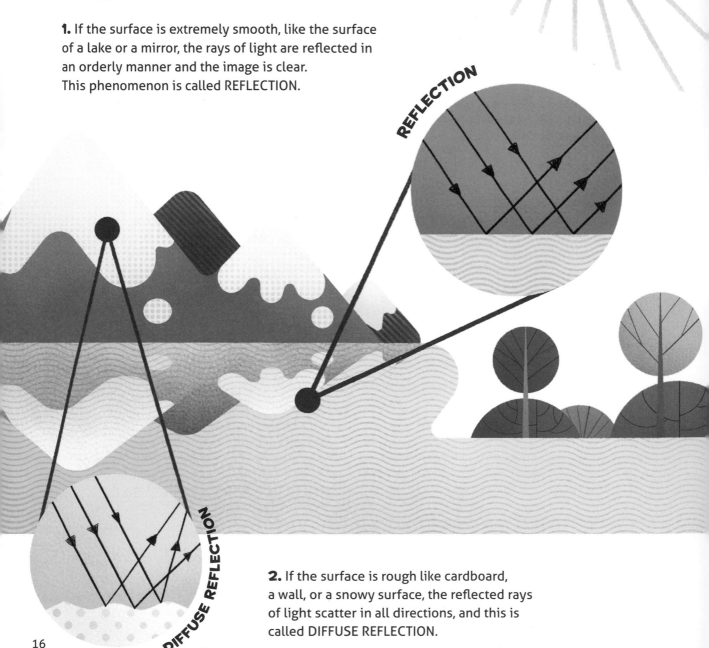

REFLECTION

DIFFUSE REFLECTION

2. If the surface is rough like cardboard, a wall, or a snowy surface, the reflected rays of light scatter in all directions, and this is called DIFFUSE REFLECTION.

DID YOU KNOW...

The ancient
Egyptians discovered
that some surfaces were able to reflect a beam of
light and make it "bounce." With an ingenious system
of well-polished slabs, used like mirrors, they were
able to reflect the sun's rays and illuminate the
inside of the pyramids.

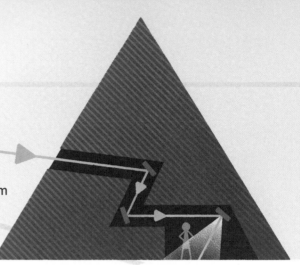

Not all of the light that hits an OPAQUE
object is reflected or scattered. Part of it
is absorbed. If the object is light-colored,
it absorbs only a small part, whereas a
dark object absorbs almost all of it.

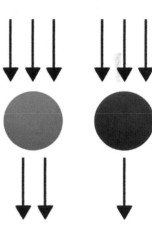

PROTECTED FROM THE SUN

When we are out in the snow
or at the beach, dark sunglass
lenses protect our eyes from
the glare caused by the
light-colored irregular surfaces,
which cause light to scatter
in all directions.

GUIDE THE LIGHT

Today, we are able to guide light through tiny fibers and use it for different purposes.

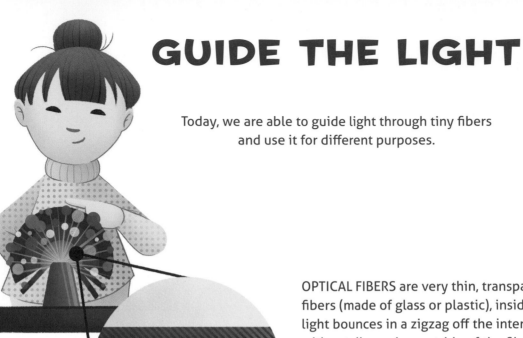

OPTICAL FIBERS are very thin, transparent fibers (made of glass or plastic), inside which light bounces in a zigzag off the internal walls without dispersing outside of the fiber.

YOU WILL NEED

- a bowl
- a transparent plastic bottle
- a thin, transparent plastic tube
- a flashlight
- Scotch tape
- modeling dough
- a dark cloth
- scissors
- water
- a thumbtack
- a dark room

HOW TO DO IT

1 Fill 3/4 of the bottle with water.

2 Use the scissors to make a hole in the lid of the bottle.

DIFFICULTY:

DIRTINESS:

TIME: 5–10 minutes

DO IT WITH:

3 Put the lid on the bottle, insert the tube into the hole, and seal it with the modeling dough.

4 Attach the flashlight to the bottom of the bottle with Scotch tape and then turn it on.

5 Wrap the bottle in the dark cloth.

WHAT HAPPENS

The jet of water that comes out of the tube is glowing! The light doesn't curve; it is reflected in a sort of zigzag down the tube until it exits.

6 Put the free end of the tube into the bowl.

With the light on, position the bottle as shown in the illustration, then pierce the bottom of the bottle with the thumbtack. The water will start to come out of the tube.

7

MIRROR, MIRROR ON THE WALL

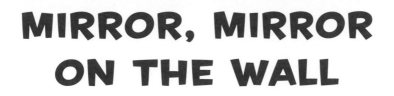

When a ray of light hits a mirror it is reflected, that is, it bounces off the surface like a ball, allowing us to see our reflection.

If the mirror is completely flat, the reflection will be the same size as the real object, although left and right are inverted.

If the mirror is curved, the reflection will be deformed, enlarged or reduced, straight, or turned upside down, depending on where the object is.

Ancient people used perfectly polished metal objects so they would have extremely smooth surfaces to look at themselves in; the mirrors we know today, made of glass and coated with a very fine layer of silver on the back, only began to appear in around 1300.

DIFFICULTY:

DIRTINESS:

TIME: *20 minutes*

DO IT WITH:

+

YOU WILL NEED

- *A4 mirror board*
- *A toy car*

1 Prop up a mirror board horizontally.

2 Put a toy car in front of it.

3 Try bending the board, first on one side and then on the other.

4 Observe the reflection of the car.

DID YOU KNOW...

Metal spoons are a practical example of mirrors that are concave and convex at the same time. Have fun looking at yourself in them and seeing how your reflection deforms.

WHAT HAPPENS

When the mirror board is bent, it acts like concave and convex mirrors. Consequently, the image of the toy car is slightly deformed.

UNDER THE SEA

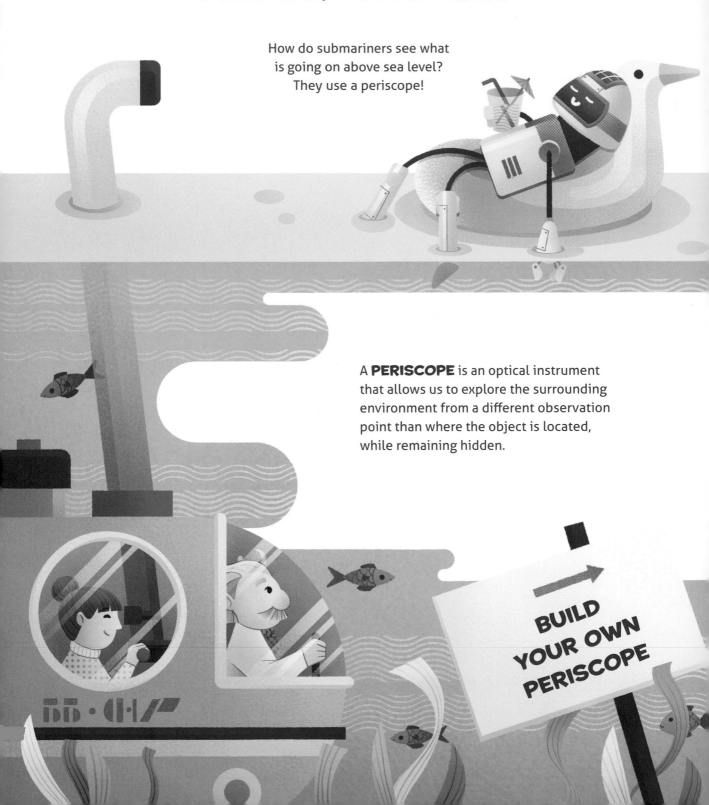

How do submariners see what
is going on above sea level?
They use a periscope!

A **PERISCOPE** is an optical instrument
that allows us to explore the surrounding
environment from a different observation
point than where the object is located,
while remaining hidden.

BUILD
YOUR OWN
PERISCOPE

HOW TO DO IT

YOU WILL NEED

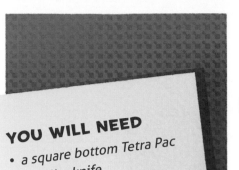

- a square bottom Tetra Pac
- a utility knife
- 2 pocket mirrors of the same size
- hot glue gun
- a pencil

1 Draw two 45° angles at each end of the Tetra Pac, as shown in the illustration.

2 Cut out the angles with the utility knife to create two slots.

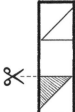

3 Using the hot glue, stick the two mirrors onto the slots so that they are facing each other.

4 Point the top mirror of the periscope toward an object on the table. Hide under the table and look at what you can see in the mirror at the bottom.

MIRROR

LIGHT

WHAT HAPPENS

The periscope works thanks to the reflection of light. Each mirror in the periscope reflects the light at an angle of 45°, equal to the angle that the light hits it.

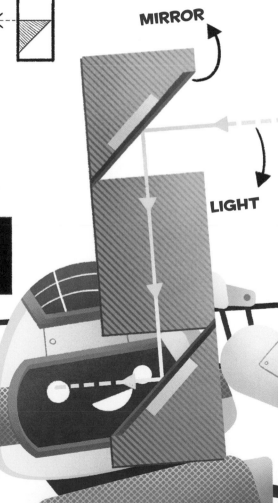

LASERDROME

A laser is a device that produces a monochromatic (single colored) beam of light. It is used for very precise measurements and surgical operations. Let's build a laser arena for hitting our target!

YOU WILL NEED

- a laser pointer
- a few small mirrors
- cardboard
- a pencil
- scissors
- Scotch tape

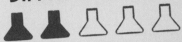

DIFFICULTY:

DIRTINESS:

TIME: 20 minutes

DO IT WITH:

HOW TO DO IT

1 Draw and cut out a cardboard circle with a diameter of 2 inches (5 cm).

2 Stick the laser onto a table with Scotch tape.

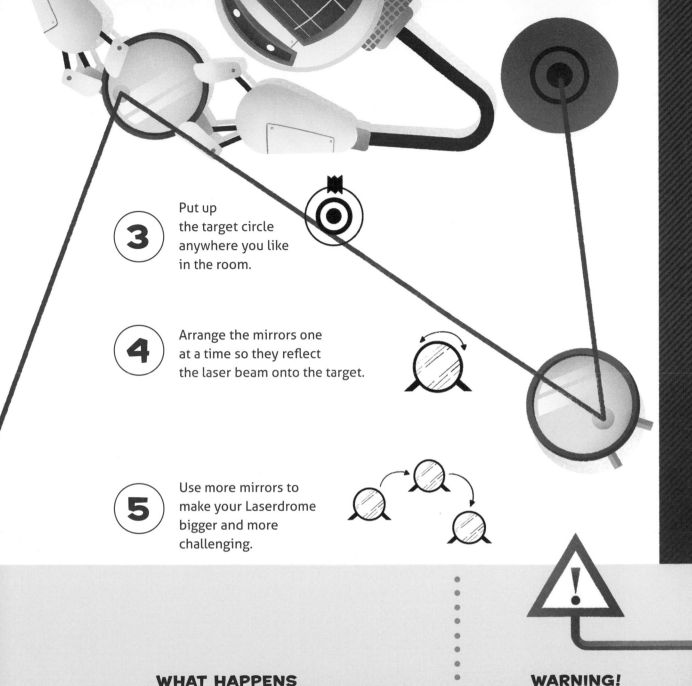

3 Put up the target circle anywhere you like in the room.

4 Arrange the mirrors one at a time so they reflect the laser beam onto the target.

5 Use more mirrors to make your Laserdrome bigger and more challenging.

WHAT HAPPENS

The laser bounces off each mirror and is reflected until it hits the target. Try building your Laserdrome in a bigger space each time.

WARNING!

Never aim the laser at people's faces.

REFRACTION

Have you ever wanted to grab an object underwater and not been able to get it because your aim was off? This happens because light passing through the water changes the way we see objects.

When light passes through two transparent mediums with different DENSITIES, like air and water or air and glass, it changes speed, which causes it to change direction. This phenomenon is called REFRACTION.

ACTUALLY, I'M HERE.

IT'S A MIRAGE

A particular phenomenon caused by the REFRACTION of light is a **mirage**. Although the classic example of this is an oasis with a pool of water in the **desert**, we are more likely to see a nonexistent puddle in the **road**.

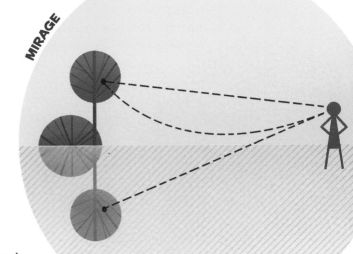

MIRAGE

On hot summer days, the air close to the ground heats up, becoming much less **dense** than the air above it. It therefore deflects the sun's rays and helps to create this phenomenon.

INCIDENT RAY

REFLECTED RAY

REFRACTED RAY

THE SECRET OF GLASSES

REFRACTION is also used in **glass lenses**, which is why we are able to correct many **defects of vision**.

27

A GLASS AND PENCIL

YOU WILL NEED
- a clear glass
- water
- a pencil

HOW TO DO IT

1 Fill the glass halfway with water.

2 Put the pencil in the water and watch what happens.

WHAT HAPPENS

The pencil appears broken, that is, the part underneath the water seems displaced with respect to the part above water. This is because the light is refracted as it passes through the air (less dense) and water (more dense), making the pencil look as if it is in a different place than where it actually is.

TURNING ARROWS

HOW TO DO IT

YOU WILL NEED

- a piece of paper
- a marker pen
- a smooth tall glass, without any decoration
- water

1 Draw an arrow on the piece of paper.

2 Put the glass in front of the piece of paper.

3 Fill the glass with water.

4 Move the glass a little at a time and watch what happens to the arrow.

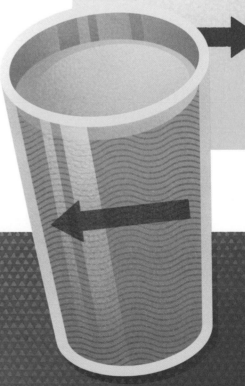

WHAT HAPPENS

After filling the glass with water, the arrow looks as if it has turned around because the glass acts as a lens.

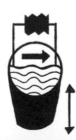

NEWTON AND LIGHT

ISAAC NEWTON discovered that when a ray of white light passes through a glass prism, it will split into several colors.

This phenomenon is called **CHROMATIC DISPERSION**.

Light is therefore a set of colors that range from red to purple. This is the visible light spectrum.

DIY RAINBOW

HOW TO DO IT

1

Cover one end of the cardboard tube with aluminum foil, then make a slit in the middle

2 Put the prism on the table next to the piece of white cardstock.

3 Create a dark space around you and put the flashlight inside the carboard tube.

4 Turn the tube so that the rays hit one side of the prism, ending up on the cardstock.

YOU WILL NEED

- a prism
- a flashlight
- a cardboard tube
- aluminum foil
- scissors
- a pin
- Scotch tape
- white cardstock

WHAT HAPPENS

You are observing the physical phenomenon called CHROMATIC DISPERSION, which is light splitting into different colors thanks to the prism.

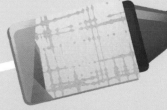

RAINBOWS IN WATER

When sunlight encounters a drop of water, a **RAINBOW** is born. The drop of water acts as a prism; it refracts the rays of light, causing their colors to disperse in a gigantic spectrum.

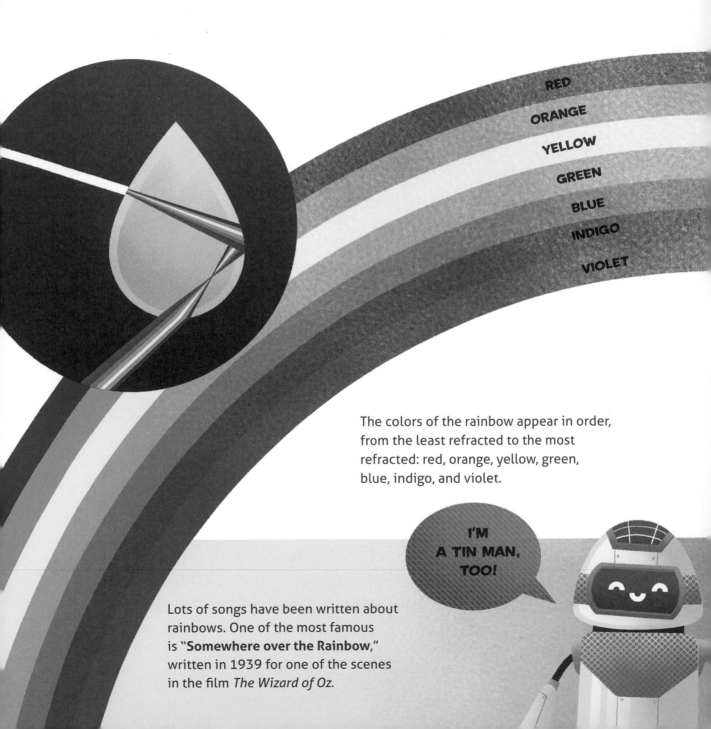

RED
ORANGE
YELLOW
GREEN
BLUE
INDIGO
VIOLET

The colors of the rainbow appear in order, from the least refracted to the most refracted: red, orange, yellow, green, blue, indigo, and violet.

I'M A TIN MAN, TOO!

Lots of songs have been written about rainbows. One of the most famous is **"Somewhere over the Rainbow,"** written in 1939 for one of the scenes in the film *The Wizard of Oz*.

HOW TO DO IT

YOU WILL NEED

- *a flashlight*
- *a shallow dish*
- *water*
- *white cardstock*
- *a mirror*

1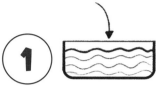
Fill the dish
with water.

2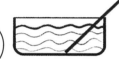
Put the mirror
in the water.

3 Shine the flashlight
on the mirror.

4 Intercept the
reflected light with
the white cardstock
and see what happens.

WHAT HAPPENS

*A rainbow forms on the cardstock. This is because
the white light reflected in the mirror is refracted as
it passes through the water and the colors that it is
composed of are deviated at different angles,
becoming visible on the cardstock.*

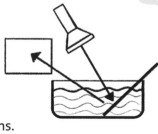

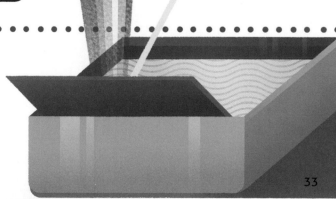

33

BEYOND THE VISIBLE SPECTRUM

The light we see and know occupies only a part of the entire ELECTROMAGNETIC SPECTRUM, or the entire range of frequencies of electromagnetic waves. This part is called the **visible spectrum**.

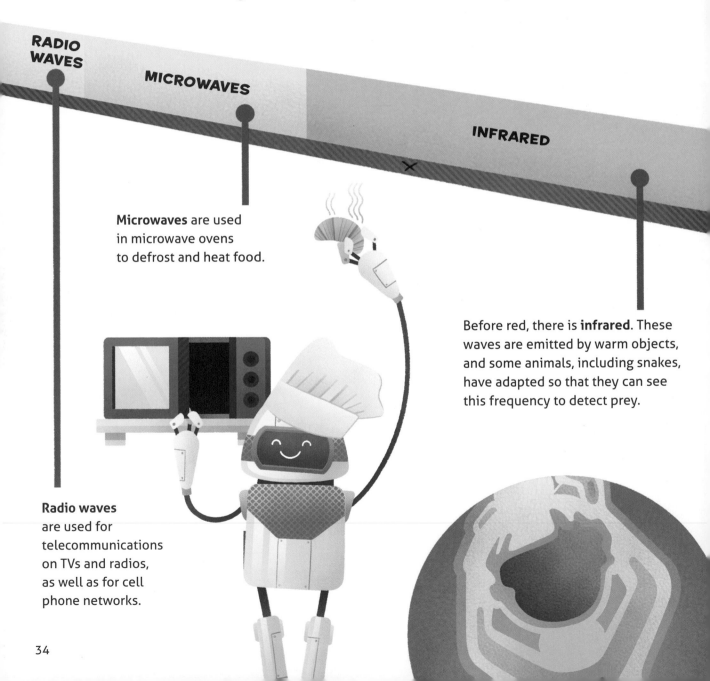

RADIO WAVES

MICROWAVES

INFRARED

Microwaves are used in microwave ovens to defrost and heat food.

Before red, there is **infrared**. These waves are emitted by warm objects, and some animals, including snakes, have adapted so that they can see this frequency to detect prey.

Radio waves are used for telecommunications on TVs and radios, as well as for cell phone networks.

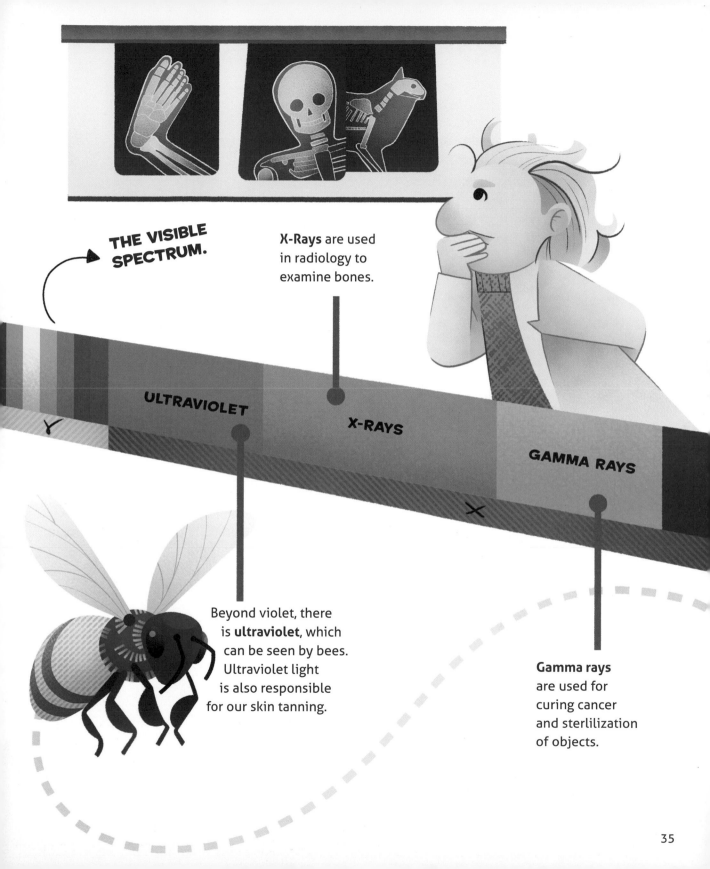

THE VISIBLE SPECTRUM.

X-Rays are used in radiology to examine bones.

ULTRAVIOLET

X-RAYS

GAMMA RAYS

Beyond violet, there is **ultraviolet**, which can be seen by bees. Ultraviolet light is also responsible for our skin tanning.

Gamma rays are used for curing cancer and sterlilization of objects.

SPECTROSCOPE

Let's make an instrument that allows you to see the separate component colors of light through a phenomenon called **diffraction**: a **spectroscope**.

YOU WILL NEED

- *a carboard tube*
- *a CD*
- *Scotch tape*
- *aluminum foil*
- *a utility knife*
- *scissors*
- *a pencil*

HOW TO DO IT

1 Make a 45° cut about one-third of the way along the tube, as shown in the illustration.

2 Using a utility knife, cut out a small square window opposite the slit.

(3) Cover the top of the tube with aluminum foil.

(4) Using a utility knife, make a small slit in the middle of the aluminum foil.

(5) Insert the CD into the 45° slit.

(6) Point the slot in the spectroscope toward the sky (not directly towards the sun), and look through the window.

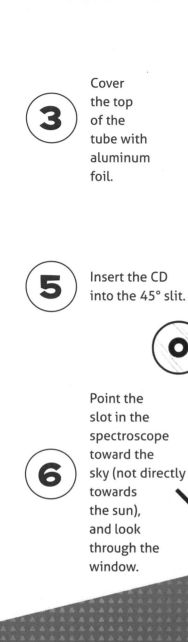

WHAT HAPPENS

When you look through the window, you will see a small rainbow forming on the CD! CDs have circular grooves that are used to record data, and they are so close together that they act as a diffraction grating that breaks down the light.

HOT BOXES

YOU WILL NEED

- 2 cardboard boxes of the same size with lids
- plastic wrap
- Scotch tape
- a cooking thermometer
- black and white poster paint
- a paint brush
- scissors
- a stopwatch

HOW TO DO IT

1 Cut a window in the top of both box lids, leaving a margin of 0.8 in (2 cm) on all sides.

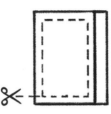

2 Paint the inside of the boxes and the lids: paint one box black and the other white; leave to dry.

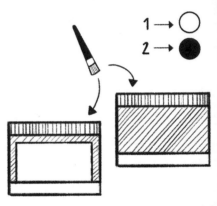

1 → ○
2 → ●

3 Cover the windows with plastic wrap and secure the edges with Scotch tape.

4 Put the white box somewhere where the transparent window is facing the sun.

5 With the pointed end of the thermometer, make a hole in one side of the box, then insert the bulb of the thermometer.

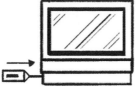

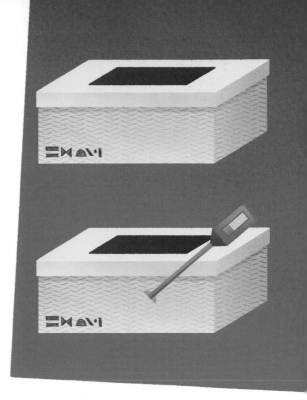

6 Make a note of the temperature every 30 seconds (10 times).

7 Repeat steps 4, 5, and 6 with the black box. Write down the different temperatures.

WHAT HAPPENS

Although at first the temperature readings for the two boxes are similar, over time the temperatures of the black box will be higher than those of the white one. This is because black absorbs light and converts it into heat, whereas white reflects it. That's why in summer we may avoid wearing black clothes and prefer wearing white!

IT'S HOT!!

INFRARED

To see beyond the **visible spectrum**, we humans need special tools.

INFRARED

Some special cameras, called **thermal imaging cameras**, can detect infrared energy, and they are used in devices for seeing in the **dark**. They are also used by **firefighters** to find their way in **smoke-filled** environments.

Astronomers use special **telescopes** that can view the sky in infrared and ultraviolet light.

Infrared light is used in **remote controls** to send signals to the **TV** or to **automatic gates**.

INFRARED AND A CELL PHONE

YOU WILL NEED

- *a cell phone*
- *a remote control with an uncovered LED light*

HOW TO DO IT

1 Go into a semi-dark or dark room, and turn on your cell phone camera.

2 Point the remote control LED light at the camera.

3 Press a button on the remote control and watch what happens.

WHAT HAPPENS

Some digital cameras have filters to block infrared light, but most of them can detect it. When you press a button on the remote control, the camera shows the LED light lighting up, and it appears on the screen as visible light.

THE SKY IN A ROOM

PHOSPHORESCENCE this is a phenomenon where certain substances continue to emit light even when they are no longer being directly illuminated.

We all know about phosphorescent stars, which absorb the light in the room and then glow in the dark for a few minutes.

In general, all products sold as being "glow-in-the-dark" are phosphorescent.

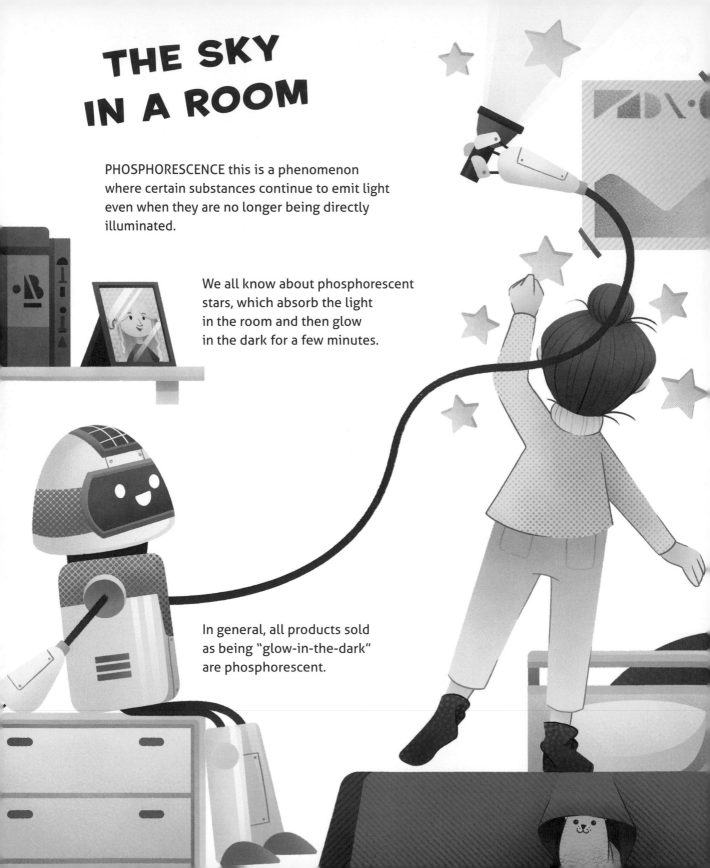

CONSTELLATIONS INDOORS

YOU WILL NEED

- a few phosphorescent stars
- a star map
- a flashlight
- an ultraviolet flashlight

HOW TO DO IT

1 Open the star map and choose a constellation.

2 Count out the right amount of stars for the constellation you chose.

3 Stick them on the wall or ceiling, with the help of an adult.

4 Turn out the lights and shine the flashlight on the stars for 10 seconds and make a note of how long the stars glow afterward.

5 Now, shine the ultraviolet flashlight on the stars for 10 seconds and make a note of how long the stars glow afterward.

WHAT HAPPENS

The stars absorb artificial and ultraviolet light differently, and therefore they re-emit the light for different lengths of time.

FLUORESCENCE!

FLUORESCENCE is the property that some substances have of **emitting light** when they are **excited**, that is, exposed to luminous radiation like **ultraviolet light**.

	💡	●
PHOSPHORESCENCE	⇒ ☼	☼
FLUORESCENCE	⇒ ☼	○

PHOSPHORESCENCE and **FLUORESCENCE** are both based on the ability of these materials and substances to **absorb energy**, get excited, and then **re-emit** it in the form of visible **light**.

The difference between the two phenomena lies in the **amount** of time they glow: While PHOSPHORESCENCE has a more lasting effect and continues even in the absence of light, FLUORESCENCE has an immediate effect and stops as soon as the exciting energy source is interrupted.

MARKER PEN

HOW TO DO IT

YOU WILL NEED

- *cardboard*
- *a marker pen*
- *an ultraviolet flashlight*

DIFFICULTY:

DIRTINESS:

TIME: *20 minutes*

DO IT WITH:

1 Draw anything you like on the cardboard with the marker pen.

2 Make the room dark.

3 Switch on the ultraviolet flashlight and shine it on the cardboard. What do you see?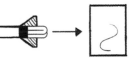

WHAT HAPPENS

The ultraviolet rays of the flashlight excite the fluorescent substance in the marker pen, which re-emits this energy in the form of visible light.

GLOSSARY

CHROMATIC DISPERSION: Phenomenon that causes light to separate into its different component colors. It is the basis for the formation of a rainbow.

DENSITY: The ratio of the mass of an object to its volume.

DIFFUSE REFLECTION: Phenomenon whereby when a beam of light encounters a rough surface, the rays are reflected in all directions, or diffused.

ELECTROMAGNETIC SPECTRUM: The entire range of component colors in sunlight. One part, called the visible spectrum, includes the colors that can be perceived by the human eye; other parts are invisible to us, such as ultraviolet (UV) or infrared rays.

FLUORESCENCE: Characteristic of certain substances to emit light after they have been exposed to luminous radiation. It differs from phosphorescence in that the object stops emitting light as soon as the external energy source is interrupted.

LUMINOUS OBJECT: An object that emits its own light.

OPAQUE: Describes an object that doesn't let light pass through, so you cannot see through it.

OPTICAL FIBERS: Very thin and transparent glass or plastic fibers inside which light bounces in a zigzag off the internal walls, without dispersing outside of the fibers.

PHOSPHORESCENCE: Characteristic of certain substances to emit light after they have been exposed to luminous radiation. It differs from fluorescence in that an object continues to emit light after it has been exposed.

REFLECTION: Phenomenon whereby when a beam of light encounters an object with a smooth and polished surface, the rays of light bounce off it and are reflected in the same direction in an orderly manner.

REFRACTION: Phenomenon whereby a ray of light undergoes a deviation when passing through one object or medium to another with a different density.

TRANSLUCENT: Describes an object that lets light partially pass through it, so you cannot see things behind it clearly.

TRANSPARENT: Describes an object that lets light pass through it, so you can see through it.

VALERIA BARATTINI

Valeria holds a master's degree in Economics and Management of Arts and Cultural Activities from the University of Ca' Foscari in Venice, and a master's in Standards for Museum Education from the Roma Tre University. She works in education and cultural planning. Since 2015, she has been working in partnership with Fosforo, holding events and activities in the field of scientific dissemination and informal teaching.

MATTIA CRIVELLINI

A graduate of Computer Science at the University of Bologna, Mattia has been studying Cognitive Sciences in the United States at Indiana University. Since 2011, he has been the director of Fosforo, the science festival of Senigallia. He organizes and plans activities, conferences, and shows for communication and dissemination of science in Italy and abroad through the NEXT Cultural Association.

ALESSANDRO GNUCCI

A science communicator and tutor, with over fifteen years of experience. In 2011, he founded Fosforo, the science festival in Senigallia, and in 2014, the Cultural Association NEXT. He designs science communication formats, and organises shows together with his colleagues at the PSIQUADRO association.

FRANCESCA GORINI

After obtaining a master's degree in Industrial Biotechnology from the University of Urbino "Carlo Bo" and doing an internship in Cambridge (UK), Francesca obtained a PhD in Molecular Medicine at the Vita Salute San Raffaele University in Milan. She has dedicated herself to research in various laboratories and to the management of clinical studies in hospitals. She teaches in schools and collaborates with Fosforo in scientific dissemination.

ROSSELLA TRIONFETTI

After graduating in Applied Arts, Rossella specialized in the field of illustration and graphics by attending various courses with professionals in the sector, including at the Mimaster of Milan. Currently, she works as an illustrator of children's books and also collaborates in the creation of apps. In recent years, she has illustrated several books for White Star Kids.

Valeria, Mattia, Alessandro, Francesca and Rossella are all part of

FOSFORO: THE SCIENCE FESTIVAL.

Fosforo: It's a fair, a festival, a meeting place. It's a series of events to give stimuli, overturn the commonplace, make people fall in love with science, and stimulate them to dream, think, invent, and discover. *Fosforo*: It's scientific dissemination. An event with national and international guests, who, since 2011, have been animating Senigallia, in the Marche region of Italy, for four days in May. This is done with surprising scientific exhibitions, laboratories, and conferences on the main scientific topics.

WSKids
WHITE STAR KIDS

White Star Kids™ is a trademark of White Star s.r.l.

© 2020 White Star s.r.l.
Piazzale Luigi Cadorna, 6 - 20123 Milan, Italy
www.whitestar.it

Translation: TperTradurre, Rome, Italy
Editing: Michele Suchomel-Casey

ISBN 978-88-544-1728-1
2 3 4 5 6   28 27 26 25 24

Printed in China

MIX
Paper from responsible sources
FSC® C178000
www.fsc.org